When Happiness Had a Holiday: Helping Families Improve and Strengthen their Relationships

This beautifully illustrated therapeutic storybook has been designed to support children and families to strengthen their relationships using solution-focused brief therapy. Healthy and supportive family relationships are essential to mental health, and as referrals to Child and Adolescent Mental Health Services continue to rise, growing research demonstrates the benefit of involving families in the treatment of children and young people facing emotional and mental health difficulties. The storybook explores the struggles faced by a typical family in which relationships have become more tense and conflictual. It can be used to spark discussion about the struggles faced by a family, and the ways in which these struggles can be overcome when they work together.

This book features:

- An engaging story with attractive illustrations, enabling difficult issues to be explored in a child-friendly manner
- An accessible and relateable narrative that allows for a discussion of family difficulties without assigning blame
- Several suggestions for practical steps that can be taken to allow happiness to return to a family.

This is a vital resource for social workers, counsellors, mental health professionals and individual and family psychotherapists working with families and children. Also available is an accompanying workbook with resources and activities: *When Happiness Had a Holiday: Helping Families Improve and Strengthen their Relationships: A Professional Resource.*

Maeve McColgan has worked for almost 30 years across a range of settings in social care and mental health. She initially qualified as a social worker and subsequently as a Family and Systemic Psychotherapist (Family Therapist). She has worked in a variety of Child and Adolescent Mental Health Services since then.

Eileen McLaughlin is currently working as a freelance Graphic Designer/ Illustrator. She has more than 25 years' experience in Visual Communication. Although she has a vast experience in a range of Design & Communication, she has a particular interest in visually assisting the development of children in the early years. Her work is published and printed in the UK, Ireland and beyond.

This is Maeve and Eileen's second collaboration, having previously published *When Worry Came to Visit*, in 2014.

the
HEALTHY
MIND *series*

©2021
Written by Maeve McColgan
Illustrated by Eileen McLaughlin

When happiness had a holiday

Helping Families Improve and Strengthen their Relationships

A Therapeutic Storybook

Written by Maeve McColgan
Illustrated by Eileen McLaughlin

When happiness had a holiday

First published 2021
by Routledge
2 Park Square, Milton Park, Abingdon, Oxon OX14 4RN

and by Routledge
52 Vanderbilt Avenue, New York, NY 10017

Routledge is an imprint of the Taylor & Francis Group, an informa business

British Library Cataloguing-in-Publication Data
A catalogue record for this book is available from the British Library

Library of Congress Cataloging-in-Publication Data
Names: McColgan, Maeve, author. | McLaughlin, Eileen, illustrator.
Title: When happiness had a holiday : Helping Families Improve and
Strengthen their Relationships : a therapeutic storybook / Maeve McColgan; illustrated by Eileen McLaughlin.
Description: Abingdon, Oxon ; New York, NY : Routledge, 2020.
Identifiers: LCCN 2019057223 (print) | LCCN 2019057224 (ebook) |
ISBN 9780367473778 (paperback) | ISBN 9781003035190 (ebook)
Subjects: LCSH: Families--Psychological aspects--Juvenile literature. |
Communication in families--Juvenile literature. | Interpersonal
conflict--Juvenile literature. | Interpersonal relations--Juvenile literature.
Classification: LCC HQ728 .M354185 2020 (print) | LCC HQ728 (ebook) | DDC 158.2/4--dc23
LC record available at https://lccn.loc.gov/2019057223
LC ebook record available at https://lccn.loc.gov/2019057224

ISBN: 978-0-367-47377-8 (pbk)
ISBN: 978-1-003-03519-0 (ebk)

Typeset in Myraid Pro
by Integra Software Services Pvt. Ltd.

'Now, stay in your room until you've got rid of that attitude.'
Sophie was really fed up. It was Saturday morning and she was in her bedroom after a big argument with her mum.

She was always getting shouted at these days for her 'attitude' – whatever that was.

Saturday mornings used to be about playing and having fun. It all changed when her dad lost his job and her mum started to get sick sometimes. Happiness seemed to take a holiday from their family while shouting moved in and took its place.

Sophie remembered when things were different, not just for her, but for her big sister Maria and her little brother Jack too. Her dad used to be a lot of fun and do things with them. Her mum used to join in their games and laugh lots. Now shouting was never far away and seemed able to get all of them to join in with it.

Later that day Sophie was playing with her friends Katie and Mai. They noticed that she was quieter than usual. 'Are you okay?' asked Katie.
Sophie told them about the changes at home and how shouting had moved in and was stopping them having good times together. Her friends tried to cheer her up, but it didn't really work.

When she got home she saw that her grandma had called in. Her mum and grandma stopped talking when Sophie joined them, but her mum looked as if she had been crying and Sophie guessed that they had been talking about all the shouting in the family. Sophie's grandma tried to chat with her, but Sophie didn't feel like talking, so she mumbled an excuse and went to find Maria.

That evening they all went to Grandma's house for dinner. She had cooked one of her great stews. While they were eating, Mum explained how upset she was that shouting had become so much a part of their family life.
She said that she thought no one else liked it either and they all agreed.
Grandma wondered if they could try to work together to find ways to get the better of shouting.

Dad said he thought they really needed to try something as shouting was with them too often. Grandma asked: 'What does shouting stop you doing?' Sophie said, 'playing together!' Maria said, 'having fun!' and Dad added 'talking.' Grandma said: 'Those sound like good things to get back into your family.'

HAVE FUN

Then she said:

'Let's think about how you would like things to be. What would you each want to be doing if you were talking and laughing, instead of shouting?'

Everyone had lots of ideas which included trips to the park, a movie night with popcorn and a family outing. Grandma asked them to think about little everyday things too.

Dad said he would like to bake a cake with the children, for mum's birthday. Mum said she would like to read bedtime stories to the children, like she used to. Sophie and Jack agreed they would like to spend more time playing together with their Lego while Maria wanted the others to play football with her.

Jack said: 'Now we just have to do it!', and they all laughed.

Sophie said: 'Well we used to be able to do it.'

Grandma asked: 'Can anyone think of recent times when shouting didn't win and you did something different?'

It was quiet for a moment while they all thought about this.

Sophie said:'What about yesterday when Jack was starting to get cross and dad began a game of hide and seek? I helped Jack hide in the laundry basket!' 'Yes', Dad said, 'I had to give up as I couldn't find him anywhere!'

Mum remembered: 'A couple of nights ago I was feeling cross that the kitchen was a mess. Maria, you told me a joke which made me laugh and then helped me tidy up. With your help, I felt much better.'

Maria said: 'Last weekend I started to shout at Sophie as I thought she'd taken my favourite necklace.' And Sophie said: 'When you realised I hadn't, you said sorry and let me borrow it the next day!'

Okay', Grandma said, 'so you agree that you want to get shouting out of your family. You know what you would like to be doing instead and you can even think of times recently when you got the better of it and did something different. So, what can you do to really get rid of shouting and get happiness to come back?'

They were all quiet. After a little time, Grandma said: 'Could you each try to do one thing differently to make shouting weaker, but not tell each other? Then in a few days time you can see if you all noticed what each of you did?' Everyone thought this might be a fun game and agreed to have a family chat the following weekend to see how things had gone. Grandma said that she knew they could make a really strong team. She added that all teams need good supporters and she'd like to help out in any way she could.

WORK TOGETHER FAMILY GAME

The next weekend they talked about their week. They agreed that while there had been some shouting, there was definitely less than the previous week. The children had all enjoyed Dad playing outdoors with them. Mum had noticed that Maria told her jokes some days, which made her laugh, Sophie had listened more and Jack had tidied his toys away more often. Maria noticed Mum was trying not to shout about untidiness and thought that earlier that day they had baked their best ever muffins together!

They were still talking when Grandma called in. Everyone told her about the many times in the last week when they had got the better of shouting. Grandma cheered! They decided to go on a family outing the following weekend and asked Grandma to join them for a trip to the zoo.

let's get happy!

Mon	☑	Told jokes
Tues	☑	Played football
Wed	☑	Walked in the park
Thurs	☑	Played a game
Fri	☑	Movie Night
Sat	☑	Baked Muffins
Sun	☑	Went to the beach

REWARD>>>> The ZOO!!

By the following weekend everyone in the family realised that shouting had made a bit of a comeback. When Grandma came to join them for the trip to the zoo, Mum was shouting at Sophie for her 'attitude'.

Grandma got everyone together and said: 'I know you are stronger than the shouting, and wonder if you've forgotten that you need to work together as a team? This week why don't you all watch each other and notice what everyone does that helps to keep shouting away. Now let's have a team hug and get to the zoo!'

HAPPY FAMILY

Sophie and her family went to Grandma's house for dinner the following weekend. Grandma listened as they all told her about the many things they had noticed that had helped to keep shouting away. These included spending more time together doing things they enjoyed, everyone helping out with household chores, and remembering to 'press the pause button' before they spoke, if they were feeling cross!

Grandma said: 'What a team! Keep on doing all the things that are working. Remember, there will be times when things feel tough and shouting tries to creep back in again, but if you work together you can get the better of it. When you're feeling stuck, do something different! I'll always help you in any way I can.'

Sophie and her family discovered that Grandma was right. By continuing to do all the things which encouraged happiness to hang around, they could keep shouting away. Sometimes shouting did try and creep back into the family, but as soon as they noticed this they would work together to get the better of it.

They found it helpful to remember Grandma's advice to 'do something different' when they were feeling stuck. At these times, they would get together and come up with new ideas. This usually helped them to show shouting the door and encourage happiness to come back from holiday, so that they could enjoy family life once more.